This Planner Belongs to

We would love to hear from you!

SIGNUP for a FREE Gift!

majestic.ontrapages.com

FOLLOW us on Instagram!

@majestic.notebooks

Questions and Customer Service

majesticnotebooks@gmail.com

Majestic
NOTEBOOKS

Notes

2021 Calendar

January

SUN	MON	TUE	WED	THU	FRI	SAT
					1	2
3	4	5	6	7	8	9
10	11	12	13	14	15	16
17	18	19	20	21	22	23
24	25	26	27	28	29	30
31						

February

SUN	MON	TUE	WED	THU	FRI	SAT
	1	2	3	4	5	6
7	8	9	10	11	12	13
14	15	16	17	18	19	20
21	22	23	24	25	26	27
28						

March

SUN	MON	TUE	WED	THU	FRI	SAT
	1	2	3	4	5	6
7	8	9	10	11	12	13
14	15	16	17	18	19	20
21	22	23	24	25	26	27
28	29	30	31			

April

SUN	MON	TUE	WED	THU	FRI	SAT
				1	2	3
4	5	6	7	8	9	10
11	12	13	14	15	16	17
18	19	20	21	22	23	24
25	26	27	28	29	30	

May

SUN	MON	TUE	WED	THU	FRI	SAT
						1
2	3	4	5	6	7	8
9	10	11	12	13	14	15
16	17	18	19	20	21	22
23	24	25	26	27	28	29
30	31					

June

SUN	MON	TUE	WED	THU	FRI	SAT
		1	2	3	4	5
6	7	8	9	10	11	12
13	14	15	16	17	18	19
20	21	22	23	24	25	26
27	28	29	30			

July

SUN	MON	TUE	WED	THU	FRI	SAT
				1	2	3
4	5	6	7	8	9	10
11	12	13	14	15	16	17
18	19	20	21	22	23	24
25	26	27	28	29	30	31

August

SUN	MON	TUE	WED	THU	FRI	SAT
1	2	3	4	5	6	7
8	9	10	11	12	13	14
15	16	17	18	19	20	21
22	23	24	25	26	27	28
29	30	31				

September

SUN	MON	TUE	WED	THU	FRI	SAT
			1	2	3	4
5	6	7	8	9	10	11
12	13	14	15	16	17	18
19	20	21	22	23	24	25
26	27	28	29	30		

October

SUN	MON	TUE	WED	THU	FRI	SAT
					1	2
3	4	5	6	7	8	9
10	11	12	13	14	15	16
17	18	19	20	21	22	23
24	25	26	27	28	29	30
31						

November

SUN	MON	TUE	WED	THU	FRI	SAT
	1	2	3	4	5	6
7	8	9	10	11	12	13
14	15	16	17	18	19	20
21	22	23	24	25	26	27
28	29	30				

December

SUN	MON	TUE	WED	THU	FRI	SAT
			1	2	3	4
5	6	7	8	9	10	11
12	13	14	15	16	17	18
19	20	21	22	23	24	25
26	27	28	29	30	31	

2021 *Holidays*

This planner features US and Canada (CA) legal holidays, important observances of major world religions and some fun days as well. *The holidays listed in this planner are accurate to be best of our knowledge and research.*

JANUARY

1   New Year's Day
5   National Keto Day
18 Martin Luther King Jr. Day
19 National Popcorn Day

FEBRUARY

2   Groundhog Day
6   Eat Ice Cream for Breakfast Day
7   Super Bowl
12 Chinese New Year
14 Valentine's Day
15 Presidents' Day
    National Flag of Canada Day
16 Mardi Gras
17 Ash Wednesday, Lent Begins

MARCH

8   International Women's Day
14 Daylight Saving Time Started
17 St. Patrick's Day
23 Puppy Day
28 Passover (First day)
29 Holi

APRIL

1   April Fool's Day
2   Good Friday
4   Easter Sunday
5   Easter Monday (CA)
13 First Day of Ramadan
20 Look Alike Day
22 Earth Day

MAY

1   May Day
5   Cinco de Mayo
6   National Nurses Day
9   Mother's Day
13 Eid al-Fitr
15 Armed Forces Day
17 Shavuot
20 Be a Millionaire Day
24 Victoria Day (CA)
31 Memorial Day

JUNE

5   World Environment Day
6   D-Day
8   Best Friends Day
14 Flag Day
19 Juneteenth
20 Father's Day
24 Swim a Lap Day

JULY

1   Canada Day
3   International Plastic Bag Free Day
4   Independence Day
5   Independence Day Observed
18 Ice Cream Day
20 Eid al-Adha
25 Parents' Day
30 National Cheesecake Day

AUGUST

1   Sisters' Day
2   Civic Holiday (CA)
7   Purple Heart Day
10 Muharram
16 Tell a Joke Day
26 Women's Equality Day

SEPTEMBER

5   Cheese Pizza Day
6   Labor Day (USA, CA)
7   Rosh Hashana
11 Patriot Day
12 National Grandparents Day
16 Yom Kippur
21 First Day of Sukkot
25 Comic Book Day

OCTOBER

4   Taco Day
11 Columbus Day
    Indigenous People's Day
    Thanksgiving Day (CA)
15 Boss's Day
18 Chocolate Cupcake Day
19 The Prophet's Birthday
31 Halloween

NOVEMBER

2   Election Day
4   Diwali, Men Make Dinner Day
7   Daylight Saving Time Ends
11 Veterans Day, Remembrance Day (CA)
18 Use Less Stuff Day
20 Universal Children's Day
25 Thanksgiving Day
26 Black Friday
28 First Sunday of Advent
29 Chanukah/Hanukkah (First day)

DECEMBER

5   Day of the Ninja
7   Pearl Harbor Remembrance Day
12 Gingerbread House Day
24 Christmas Observed
25 Christmas
26 Kwanzaa Begins, Boxing Day (CA, UK)
31 New Year's Eve

01

JANUARY
2021

December

SUN	MON	TUE	WED	THU	FRI	SAT
		1	2	3	4	5
6	7	8	9	10	11	12
13	14	15	16	17	18	19
20	21	22	23	24	25	26
27	28	29	30	31		

Major Goals

- ☐ _____
- ☐ _____
- ☐ _____
- ☐ _____
- ☐ _____
- ☐ _____
- ☐ _____
- ☐ _____

Notes

Important Dates

SUNDAY	MONDAY	TUESDAY
31		
03	04	05 National Keto Day
10	11	12
17	18 Martin Luther King Jr. Day	19 National Popcorn Day
24	25	26

February

SUN	MON	TUE	WED	THU	FRI	SAT
	1	2	3	4	5	6
7	8	9	10	11	12	13
14	15	16	17	18	19	20
21	22	23	24	25	26	27
28						

In order to be irreplaceable one must always be different

- Coco Chanel

WEDNESDAY	THURSDAY	FRIDAY	SATURDAY
		01 New Year's Day	02
06	07	08	09
13	14	15	16
20	21	22	23
27	28	29	30

02

FEBRUARY
2021

January

SUN	MON	TUE	WED	THU	FRI	SAT
					1	2
3	4	5	6	7	8	9
10	11	12	13	14	15	16
17	18	19	20	21	22	23
24	25	26	27	28	29	30
31						

Major Goals

- [ ]
- [ ]
- [ ]
- [ ]
- [ ]
- [ ]
- [ ]
- [ ]

Notes

Important Dates

SUNDAY	MONDAY	TUESDAY
	01	02 Groundhog Day
07 Super Bowl	08	09
14 Valentine's Day	15 Presidents' Day / National Flag of Canada Day	16 Mardi Gras
21	22	23
28		

March

SUN	MON	TUE	WED	THU	FRI	SAT
		1	2	3	4	5	6
7	8	9	10	11	12	13
14	15	16	17	18	19	20
21	22	23	24	25	26	27
28	29	30	31			

Love is not an emotion, it's your very existence

- Rumi

WEDNESDAY	THURSDAY	FRIDAY	SATURDAY
03	04	05	06 Eat Ice Cream for Breakfast Day
10	11	12 Chinese New Year	13
17 Ash Wednesday Lent Begins	18	19	20
24	25	26	27

03

MARCH
2021

February

SUN	MON	TUE	WED	THU	FRI	SAT
	1	2	3	4	5	6
7	8	9	10	11	12	13
14	15	16	17	18	19	20
21	22	23	24	25	26	27
28						

Major Goals

- [ ] _____
- [ ] _____
- [ ] _____
- [ ] _____
- [ ] _____
- [ ] _____
- [ ] _____
- [ ] _____

Notes

Important Dates

SUNDAY	MONDAY	TUESDAY
	01	02
07	08 International Women's Day	09
14 Daylight Saving Time Started	15	16
21	22	23 Puppy Day
28 Passover	29 Holi	30

April

SUN	MON	TUE	WED	THU	FRI	SAT
				1	2	3
4	5	6	7	8	9	10
11	12	13	14	15	16	17
18	19	20	21	22	23	24
25	26	27	28	29	30	

She believed she could, so she did

- Unknown

WEDNESDAY	THURSDAY	FRIDAY	SATURDAY
03	04	05	06
10	11	12	13
17 St. Patrick's Day	18	19	20
24	25	26	27
31			

04

APRIL
2021

March

SUN	MON	TUE	WED	THU	FRI	SAT
	1	2	3	4	5	6
7	8	9	10	11	12	13
14	15	16	17	18	19	20
21	22	23	24	25	26	27
28	29	30	31			

Major Goals

☐ _____
☐ _____
☐ _____
☐ _____
☐ _____
☐ _____
☐ _____
☐ _____

Notes

Important Dates

SUNDAY	MONDAY	TUESDAY
04 — Easter Sunday	05 — Easter Monday (CA)	06
11	12	13 — First Day of Ramadan
18	19	20 — Look Alike Day
25	26	27

May

SUN	MON	TUE	WED	THU	FRI	SAT
						1
2	3	4	5	6	7	8
9	10	11	12	13	14	15
16	17	18	19	20	21	22
23	24	25	26	27	28	29
30	31					

No act of kindness, no matter how small, is ever wasted

- Aesop

WEDNESDAY	THURSDAY	FRIDAY	SATURDAY
	01 April Fool's Day	02 Good Friday	03
07	08	09	10
14	15	16	17
21	22 Earth Day	23	24
28	29	30	

05

MAY
2021

April

SUN	MON	TUE	WED	THU	FRI	SAT
				1	2	3
4	5	6	7	8	9	10
11	12	13	14	15	16	17
18	19	20	21	22	23	24
25	26	27	28	29	30	

Major Goals

- ☐ _____
- ☐ _____
- ☐ _____
- ☐ _____
- ☐ _____
- ☐ _____
- ☐ _____
- ☐ _____

Notes

Important Dates

SUNDAY	MONDAY	TUESDAY
30	31 Memorial Day	
02	03	04
09 Mother's Day	10	11
16	17 Shavuot	18
23	24 Victoria Day (CA)	25

June

SUN	MON	TUE	WED	THU	FRI	SAT
			1	2	3	4	5
6	7	8	9	10	11	12
13	14	15	16	17	18	19
20	21	22	23	24	25	26
27	28	29	30			

Doubt kills more dreams than failure ever will

- Suzy Kassem

WEDNESDAY	THURSDAY	FRIDAY	SATURDAY
			01 May Day
05 Cinco de Mayo	06 National Nurses Day	07	08
12	13 Eid al-Fitr	14	15 Armed Forces Day
19	20 Be a Millionaire Day	21	22
26	27	28	29

06

JUNE
2021

May

SUN	MON	TUE	WED	THU	FRI	SAT
						1
2	3	4	5	6	7	8
9	10	11	12	13	14	15
16	17	18	19	20	21	22
23	24	25	26	27	28	29
30	31					

Major Goals

☐ _____
☐ _____
☐ _____
☐ _____
☐ _____
☐ _____
☐ _____
☐ _____

Notes

Important Dates

SUNDAY	MONDAY	TUESDAY
		01
06 — D-Day	07	08 — Best Friends Day
13	14 — Flag Day	15
20 — Father's Day	21	22
27	28	29

July

SUN	MON	TUE	WED	THU	FRI	SAT
				1	2	3
4	5	6	7	8	9	10
11	12	13	14	15	16	17
18	19	20	21	22	23	24
25	26	27	28	29	30	31

Always, always have a plan

- Rick Riordan

WEDNESDAY	THURSDAY	FRIDAY	SATURDAY
02	03	04	05 World Environment Day
09	10	11	12
16	17	18	19 Juneteenth
23	24 Swim a Lap Day	25	26
30			

07

June

SUN	MON	TUE	WED	THU	FRI	SAT
		1	2	3	4	5
6	7	8	9	10	11	12
13	14	15	16	17	18	19
20	21	22	23	24	25	26
27	28	29	30			

Major Goals

- [ ] _____
- [ ] _____
- [ ] _____
- [ ] _____
- [ ] _____
- [ ] _____
- [ ] _____
- [ ] _____

Notes

Important Dates

SUNDAY	MONDAY	TUESDAY
04 Independence Day	05 Independence Day Observed	06
11	12	13
18 Ice Cream Day	19	20 Eid al-Adha
25 Parents' Day	26	27

August

SUN	MON	TUE	WED	THU	FRI	SAT
1	2	3	4	5	6	7
8	9	10	11	12	13	14
15	16	17	18	19	20	21
22	23	24	25	26	27	28
29	30	31				

I think everybody should focus on inner beauty

- Paloma Faith

WEDNESDAY	THURSDAY	FRIDAY	SATURDAY
	01 Canada Day	02	03 International Plastic Bag Free Day
07	08	09	10
14	15	16	17
21	22	23	24
28	29	30 National Cheesecake Day	31

08

AUGUST
2021

July

SUN	MON	TUE	WED	THU	FRI	SAT
				1	2	3
4	5	6	7	8	9	10
11	12	13	14	15	16	17
18	19	20	21	22	23	24
25	26	27	28	29	30	31

Major Goals

- ☐ _____
- ☐ _____
- ☐ _____
- ☐ _____
- ☐ _____
- ☐ _____
- ☐ _____
- ☐ _____

Notes

Important Dates

SUNDAY	MONDAY	TUESDAY
01 Sisters' Day	02 Civic Holiday (CA)	03
08	09	10 Muharram
15	16 Tell a Joke Day	17
22	23	24
29	30	31

September

SUN	MON	TUE	WED	THU	FRI	SAT
				1	2	3	4
5	6	7	8	9	10	11
12	13	14	15	16	17	18
19	20	21	22	23	24	25
26	27	28	29	30		

Opportunities don't happen. You create them

- Chris Grosser

WEDNESDAY	THURSDAY	FRIDAY	SATURDAY
04	05	06	07 Purple Heart Day
11	12	13	14
18	19	20	21
25	26 Women's Equality Day	27	28

09

SEPTEMBER
2021

August

SUN	MON	TUE	WED	THU	FRI	SAT
1	2	3	4	5	6	7
8	9	10	11	12	13	14
15	16	17	18	19	20	21
22	23	24	25	26	27	28
29	30	31				

Major Goals

☐ _____
☐ _____
☐ _____
☐ _____
☐ _____
☐ _____
☐ _____
☐ _____

Notes

Important Dates

SUNDAY	MONDAY	TUESDAY
05 Cheese Pizza Day	06 Labor Day (USA, CA)	07 Rosh Hashana
12 National Grandparents Day	13	14
19	20	21 First Day of Sukkot
26	27	28

October

SUN	MON	TUE	WED	THU	FRI	SAT
					1	2
3	4	5	6	7	8	9
10	11	12	13	14	15	16
17	18	19	20	21	22	23
24	25	26	27	28	29	30
31						

The ability to learn is the most important quality a leader can have

- Sheryl Sandberg

WEDNESDAY	THURSDAY	FRIDAY	SATURDAY
01	02	03	04
08	09	10	11 Patriot Day
15	16 Yom Kippur	17	18
22	23	24	25 Comic Book Day
29	30		

10 OCTOBER

2021

September

SUN	MON	TUE	WED	THU	FRI	SAT
			1	2	3	4
5	6	7	8	9	10	11
12	13	14	15	16	17	18
19	20	21	22	23	24	25
26	27	28	29	30		

Major Goals

- ☐ _____
- ☐ _____
- ☐ _____
- ☐ _____
- ☐ _____
- ☐ _____
- ☐ _____
- ☐ _____

Notes

Important Dates

SUNDAY	MONDAY	TUESDAY
31 Halloween		
03	**04** Taco Day	**05**
10	**11** Columbus Day / Indigenous People's Day / Thanksgiving Day (CA)	**12**
17	**18** Chocolate Cupcake Day	**19** The Prophet's Birthday
24	**25**	**26**

November

SUN	MON	TUE	WED	THU	FRI	SAT
		1	2	3	4	5	6
7	8	9	10	11	12	13
14	15	16	17	18	19	20
21	22	23	24	25	26	27
28	29	30				

Not all those who wander are lost

- J. R. R. Tolkien

WEDNESDAY	THURSDAY	FRIDAY	SATURDAY
		01	02
06	07	08	09
13	14	15 Boss's Day	16
20	21	22	23
27	28	29	30

11

NOVEMBER
2021

October
SUN	MON	TUE	WED	THU	FRI	SAT
					1	2
3	4	5	6	7	8	9
10	11	12	13	14	15	16
17	18	19	20	21	22	23
24	25	26	27	28	29	30
31						

Major Goals

- ☐ _____
- ☐ _____
- ☐ _____
- ☐ _____
- ☐ _____
- ☐ _____
- ☐ _____
- ☐ _____

Notes

Important Dates

SUNDAY	MONDAY	TUESDAY
	01	02 Election Day
07 Daylight Saving Time Ends	08	09
14	15	16
21	22	23
28 First Sunday of Advent	29 Chanukah/Hanukkah (First day)	30

December

SUN	MON	TUE	WED	THU	FRI	SAT
				1	2	3	4
5	6	7	8	9	10	11
12	13	14	15	16	17	18
19	20	21	22	23	24	25
26	27	28	29	30	31	

Focus on being balanced – success is balance

- Laila Ali

WEDNESDAY	THURSDAY	FRIDAY	SATURDAY
03	04 Diwali Men Make Dinner Day	05	06
10	11 Veterans Day Remembrance Day (CA)	12	13
17	18 Use Less Stuff Day	19	20 Universal Children's Day
24	25 Thanksgiving Day	26 Black Friday	27

12
DECEMBER
2021

November

SUN	MON	TUE	WED	THU	FRI	SAT
	1	2	3	4	5	6
7	8	9	10	11	12	13
14	15	16	17	18	19	20
21	22	23	24	25	26	27
28	29	30				

Major Goals

- ☐ _____
- ☐ _____
- ☐ _____
- ☐ _____
- ☐ _____
- ☐ _____
- ☐ _____
- ☐ _____

Notes

Important Dates

SUNDAY	MONDAY	TUESDAY
05 Day of the Ninja	06	07 Pearl Harbor Remembrance Day
12 Gingerbread House Day	13	14
19	20	21
26 Kwanzaa Begins, Boxing Day (CA, UK)	27	28

January

SUN	MON	TUE	WED	THU	FRI	SAT
						1
2	3	4	5	6	7	8
9	10	11	12	13	14	15
16	17	18	19	20	21	22
23	24	25	26	27	28	29
30	31					

I learned the value of hard work by working hard

- Margaret Mead

WEDNESDAY	THURSDAY	FRIDAY	SATURDAY
01	02	03	04
08	09	10	11
15	16	17	18
22	23	24 — Christmas Observed	25 — Christmas
29	30	31 — New Year's Eve	

Notes

Notes

2022 Calendar

January

SUN	MON	TUE	WED	THU	FRI	SAT
						1
2	3	4	5	6	7	8
9	10	11	12	13	14	15
16	17	18	19	20	21	22
23	24	25	26	27	28	29
30	31					

February

SUN	MON	TUE	WED	THU	FRI	SAT
		1	2	3	4	5
6	7	8	9	10	11	12
13	14	15	16	17	18	19
20	21	22	23	24	25	26
27	28					

March

SUN	MON	TUE	WED	THU	FRI	SAT
		1	2	3	4	5
6	7	8	9	10	11	12
13	14	15	16	17	18	19
20	21	22	23	24	25	26
27	28	29	30	31		

April

SUN	MON	TUE	WED	THU	FRI	SAT
					1	2
3	4	5	6	7	8	9
10	11	12	13	14	15	16
17	18	19	20	21	22	23
24	25	26	27	28	29	30

May

SUN	MON	TUE	WED	THU	FRI	SAT
1	2	3	4	5	6	7
8	9	10	11	12	13	14
15	16	17	18	19	20	21
22	23	24	25	26	27	28
29	30	31				

June

SUN	MON	TUE	WED	THU	FRI	SAT
			1	2	3	4
5	6	7	8	9	10	11
12	13	14	15	16	17	18
19	20	21	22	23	24	25
26	27	28	29	30		

July

SUN	MON	TUE	WED	THU	FRI	SAT
					1	2
3	4	5	6	7	8	9
10	11	12	13	14	15	16
17	18	19	20	21	22	23
24	25	26	27	28	29	30
31						

August

SUN	MON	TUE	WED	THU	FRI	SAT
	1	2	3	4	5	6
7	8	9	10	11	12	13
14	15	16	17	18	19	20
21	22	23	24	25	26	27
28	29	30	31			

September

SUN	MON	TUE	WED	THU	FRI	SAT
				1	2	3
4	5	6	7	8	9	10
11	12	13	14	15	16	17
18	19	20	21	22	23	24
25	26	27	28	29	30	

October

SUN	MON	TUE	WED	THU	FRI	SAT
						1
2	3	4	5	6	7	8
9	10	11	12	13	14	15
16	17	18	19	20	21	22
23	24	25	26	27	28	29
30	31					

November

SUN	MON	TUE	WED	THU	FRI	SAT
		1	2	3	4	5
6	7	8	9	10	11	12
13	14	15	16	17	18	19
20	21	22	23	24	25	26
27	28	29	30			

December

SUN	MON	TUE	WED	THU	FRI	SAT
				1	2	3
4	5	6	7	8	9	10
11	12	13	14	15	16	17
18	19	20	21	22	23	24
25	26	27	28	29	30	31

2022 *Holidays*

This planner features US and Canada (CA) legal holidays, important observances of major world religions and some fun days as well. *The holidays listed in this planner are accurate to be best of our knowledge and research.*

JANUARY

- 1 New Year's Day
- 5 National Keto Day
- 17 Martin Luther King Jr. Day
- 19 National Popcorn Day

FEBRUARY

- 1 Chinese New Year
- 2 Groundhog Day
- 5 Eat Ice Cream for Breakfast Day
- 6 Super Bowl
- 14 Valentine's Day
- 15 National Flag of Canada Day
- 21 Presidents' Day

MARCH

- 1 Mardi Gras
- 2 Ash Wednesday, Lent Begins
- 8 International Women's Day
- 13 Daylight Saving Time Started
- 17 St. Patrick's Day
- 19 Holi
- 23 Puppy Day

APRIL

- 1 April Fool's Day
- 3 First Day of Ramadan
- 15 Good Friday
- 16 Passover (First day)
- 17 Easter Sunday
- 18 Easter Monday (CA)
- 20 Look Alike Day
- 22 Earth Day

MAY

- 1 May Day
- 3 Eid al-Fitr
- 5 Cinco de Mayo
- 6 National Nurses Day
- 8 Mother's Day
- 20 Be a Millionaire Day
- 21 Armed Forces Day
- 23 Victoria Day (CA)
- 30 Memorial Day

JUNE

- 5 Shavuot, World Environment Day
- 6 D-Day
- 8 Best Friends Day
- 14 Flag Day
- 19 Juneteenth, Father's Day
- 24 Swim a Lap Day

JULY

- 1 Canada Day
- 3 International Plastic Bag Free Day
- 4 Independence Day
- 10 Eid al-Adha
- 17 Ice Cream Day
- 24 Parents' Day
- 30 Muharram
- National Cheesecake Day

AUGUST

- 1 Civic Holiday (CA)
- 7 Purple Heart Day, Sisters' Day
- 16 Tell a Joke Day
- 26 Women's Equality Day

SEPTEMBER

- 5 Labor Day (USA, CA)
- Cheese Pizza Day
- 11 National Grandparents Day
- Patriot Day
- 25 Comic Book Day
- 26 Rosh Hashana

OCTOBER

- 4 Taco Day
- 5 Yom Kippur
- 8 The Prophet's Birthday
- 10 Columbus Day
- First Day of Sukkot
- Indigenous People's Day
- Thanksgiving Day (CA)
- 17 Boss's Day
- 18 Chocolate Cupcake Day
- 24 Diwali
- 31 Halloween

NOVEMBER

- 3 Men Make Dinner Day
- 6 Daylight Saving Time Ends
- 8 Election Day
- 11 Veterans Day, Remembrance Day (CA)
- 17 Use Less Stuff Day
- 20 Universal Children's Day
- 24 Thanksgiving Day
- 25 Black Friday
- 27 First Sunday of Advent

DECEMBER

- 5 Day of the Ninja
- 7 Pearl Harbor Remembrance Day
- 12 Gingerbread House Day
- 19 Chanukah/Hanukkah (First day)
- 25 Christmas
- 26 Kwanzaa Begins
- Christmas Observed
- Boxing Day (CA, UK)
- 31 New Year's Eve

01

JANUARY
2022

December

SUN	MON	TUE	WED	THU	FRI	SAT
			1	2	3	4
5	6	7	8	9	10	11
12	13	14	15	16	17	18
19	20	21	22	23	24	25
26	27	28	29	30	31	

Major Goals

- ☐ _____
- ☐ _____
- ☐ _____
- ☐ _____
- ☐ _____
- ☐ _____
- ☐ _____
- ☐ _____

Notes

Important Dates

SUNDAY	MONDAY	TUESDAY
30	31	
02	03	04
09	10	11
16	17 Martin Luther King Jr. Day	18
23	24	25

February

SUN	MON	TUE	WED	THU	FRI	SAT
		1	2	3	4	5
6	7	8	9	10	11	12
13	14	15	16	17	18	19
20	21	22	23	24	25	26
27	28					

Everything has beauty, but not everyone sees it

- Confucius

WEDNESDAY	THURSDAY	FRIDAY	SATURDAY
			01 New Year's Day
05 National Keto Day	06	07	08
12	13	14	15
19 National Popcorn Day	20	21	22
26	27	28	29

02

FEBRUARY
2022

January
SUN	MON	TUE	WED	THU	FRI	SAT
						1
2	3	4	5	6	7	8
9	10	11	12	13	14	15
16	17	18	19	20	21	22
23	24	25	26	27	28	29
30	31					

Major Goals

- ☐ _____
- ☐ _____
- ☐ _____
- ☐ _____
- ☐ _____
- ☐ _____
- ☐ _____
- ☐ _____

Notes

Important Dates

SUNDAY	MONDAY	TUESDAY
		01 Chinese New Year
06 Super Bowl	07	08
13	14 Valentine's Day	15 National Flag of Canada Day
20	21 Presidents' Day	22
27	28	

March

SUN	MON	TUE	WED	THU	FRI	SAT
		1	2	3	4	5
6	7	8	9	10	11	12
13	14	15	16	17	18	19
20	21	22	23	24	25	26
27	28	29	30	31		

Each day provides its own gifts

- Marcus Aurelius

WEDNESDAY	THURSDAY	FRIDAY	SATURDAY
02 — Groundhog Day	03	04	05 — Eat Ice Cream for Breakfast Day
09	10	11	12
16	17	18	19
23	24	25	26

03

MARCH
2022

February

SUN	MON	TUE	WED	THU	FRI	SAT
		1	2	3	4	5
6	7	8	9	10	11	12
13	14	15	16	17	18	19
20	21	22	23	24	25	26
27	28					

Major Goals

- ☐ _____
- ☐ _____
- ☐ _____
- ☐ _____
- ☐ _____
- ☐ _____
- ☐ _____
- ☐ _____

Notes

Important Dates

SUNDAY	MONDAY	TUESDAY
		01 — Mardi Gras
06	07	08 — International Women's Day
13 — Daylight Saving Time Started	14	15
20	21	22
27	28	29

April

SUN	MON	TUE	WED	THU	FRI	SAT
					1	2
3	4	5	6	7	8	9
10	11	12	13	14	15	16
17	18	19	20	21	22	23
24	25	26	27	28	29	30

Trying to be a man is a waste of a woman

– Coco Chanel

WEDNESDAY	THURSDAY	FRIDAY	SATURDAY
02 Ash Wednesday Lent Begins	03	04	05
09	10	11	12
16	17 St. Patrick's Day	18	19 Holi
23 Puppy Day	24	25	26
30	31		

04

APRIL
2022

March

SUN	MON	TUE	WED	THU	FRI	SAT
		1	2	3	4	5
6	7	8	9	10	11	12
13	14	15	16	17	18	19
20	21	22	23	24	25	26
27	28	29	30	31		

Major Goals

- ☐ _____
- ☐ _____
- ☐ _____
- ☐ _____
- ☐ _____
- ☐ _____
- ☐ _____
- ☐ _____

Notes

Important Dates

SUNDAY	MONDAY	TUESDAY
03 First Day of Ramadan	04	05
10	11	12
17 Easter Sunday	18 Easter Monday (CA)	19
24	25	26

May

SUN	MON	TUE	WED	THU	FRI	SAT
1	2	3	4	5	6	7
8	9	10	11	12	13	14
15	16	17	18	19	20	21
22	23	24	25	26	27	28
29	30	31				

Stop chasing the money and start chasing the passion

- Tony Hsieh

WEDNESDAY	THURSDAY	FRIDAY	SATURDAY
		01 April Fool's Day	02
06	07	08	09
13	14	15 Good Friday	16 Passover (First day)
20 Look Alike Day	21	22 Earth Day	23
27	28	29	30

05

MAY
2022

April

SUN	MON	TUE	WED	THU	FRI	SAT
					1	2
3	4	5	6	7	8	9
10	11	12	13	14	15	16
17	18	19	20	21	22	23
24	25	26	27	28	29	30

Major Goals

- [ ]
- [ ]
- [ ]
- [ ]
- [ ]
- [ ]
- [ ]
- [ ]

Notes

Important Dates

SUNDAY	MONDAY	TUESDAY
01 May Day	02	03 Eid al-Fitr
08 Mother's Day	09	10
15	16	17
22	23 Victoria Day (CA)	24
29	30 Memorial Day	31

June

SUN	MON	TUE	WED	THU	FRI	SAT
			1	2	3	4
5	6	7	8	9	10	11
12	13	14	15	16	17	18
19	20	21	22	23	24	25
26	27	28	29	30		

Don't let anyone ever dull your sparkle

- Unknown

WEDNESDAY	THURSDAY	FRIDAY	SATURDAY
04	05 Cinco de Mayo	06 National Nurses Day	07
11	12	13	14
18	19	20 Be a Millionaire Day	21 Armed Forces Day
25	26	27	28

06

JUNE
2022

May

SUN	MON	TUE	WED	THU	FRI	SAT
1	2	3	4	5	6	7
8	9	10	11	12	13	14
15	16	17	18	19	20	21
22	23	24	25	26	27	28
29	30	31				

Major Goals

- ☐ _____
- ☐ _____
- ☐ _____
- ☐ _____
- ☐ _____
- ☐ _____
- ☐ _____
- ☐ _____

Notes

Important Dates

SUNDAY	MONDAY	TUESDAY
05 — Shavuot / World Environment Day	06 — D-Day	07
12	13	14 — Flag Day
19 — Juneteenth / Father's Day	20	21
26	27	28

July

SUN	MON	TUE	WED	THU	FRI	SAT
					1	2
3	4	5	6	7	8	9
10	11	12	13	14	15	16
17	18	19	20	21	22	23
24	25	26	27	28	29	30
31						

Kindness is like snow- it beautifies everything it covers

\- Kahlil Gibran

WEDNESDAY	THURSDAY	FRIDAY	SATURDAY
01	02	03	04
08 Best Friends Day	09	10	11
15	16	17	18
22	23	24 Swim a Lap Day	25
29	30		

07

JULY

2022

June

SUN	MON	TUE	WED	THU	FRI	SAT
			1	2	3	4
5	6	7	8	9	10	11
12	13	14	15	16	17	18
19	20	21	22	23	24	25
26	27	28	29	30		

Major Goals

- ☐ _____
- ☐ _____
- ☐ _____
- ☐ _____
- ☐ _____
- ☐ _____
- ☐ _____
- ☐ _____

Notes

Important Dates

SUNDAY	MONDAY	TUESDAY
31		
03 International Plastic Bag Free Day	04 Independence Day	05
10 Eid al-Adha	11	12
17 Ice Cream Day	18	19
24 Parents' Day	25	26

August

SUN	MON	TUE	WED	THU	FRI	SAT
	1	2	3	4	5	6
7	8	9	10	11	12	13
14	15	16	17	18	19	20
21	22	23	24	25	26	27
28	29	30	31			

The most common way people give up their power is by
Thinking they don't have any

\- Alice Walker

WEDNESDAY	THURSDAY	FRIDAY	SATURDAY
		01 Canada Day	02
06	07	08	09
13	14	15	16
20	21	22	23
27	28	29	30 Muharram National Cheesecake Day

08

AUGUST
2022

July

SUN	MON	TUE	WED	THU	FRI	SAT
					1	2
3	4	5	6	7	8	9
10	11	12	13	14	15	16
17	18	19	20	21	22	23
24	25	26	27	28	29	30
31						

Major Goals

- ☐ _____
- ☐ _____
- ☐ _____
- ☐ _____
- ☐ _____
- ☐ _____
- ☐ _____
- ☐ _____

Notes

Important Dates

SUNDAY	MONDAY	TUESDAY
	01 Civic Holiday (CA)	02
07 Purple Heart Day, Sisters' Day	08	09
14	15	16 Tell a Joke Day
21	22	23
28	29	30

September

SUN	MON	TUE	WED	THU	FRI	SAT
					1	2	3
4	5	6	7	8	9	10
11	12	13	14	15	16	17
18	19	20	21	22	23	24
25	26	27	28	29	30	

A journey of a thousand miles must begin with a single step

- Lao Tzu

WEDNESDAY	THURSDAY	FRIDAY	SATURDAY
03	04	05	06
10	11	12	13
17	18	19	20
24	25	26 Women's Equality Day	27
31			

09

SEPTEMBER
2022

August

SUN	MON	TUE	WED	THU	FRI	SAT
	1	2	3	4	5	6
7	8	9	10	11	12	13
14	15	16	17	18	19	20
21	22	23	24	25	26	27
28	29	30	31			

Major Goals

- ☐ _____
- ☐ _____
- ☐ _____
- ☐ _____
- ☐ _____
- ☐ _____
- ☐ _____
- ☐ _____

Notes

Important Dates

SUNDAY	MONDAY	TUESDAY
04	05 Labor Day (USA, CA) Cheese Pizza Day	06
11 National Grandparents Day Patriot Day	12	13
18	19	20
25 Comic Book Day	26 Rosh Hashana	27

October

SUN	MON	TUE	WED	THU	FRI	SAT
						1
2	3	4	5	6	7	8
9	10	11	12	13	14	15
16	17	18	19	20	21	22
23	24	25	26	27	28	29
30	31					

When i am with you, everything is prayer

- Rumi

WEDNESDAY	THURSDAY	FRIDAY	SATURDAY
	01	02	03
07	08	09	10
14	15	16	17
21	22	23	24
28	29	30	

10 OCTOBER
2022

September

SUN	MON	TUE	WED	THU	FRI	SAT
				1	2	3
4	5	6	7	8	9	10
11	12	13	14	15	16	17
18	19	20	21	22	23	24
25	26	27	28	29	30	

Major Goals

- ☐ _____
- ☐ _____
- ☐ _____
- ☐ _____
- ☐ _____
- ☐ _____
- ☐ _____
- ☐ _____

Notes

Important Dates

SUNDAY	MONDAY	TUESDAY
30	31 — Halloween	
02	03	04 — Taco Day
09	10 — Columbus Day / First Day of Sukkot / Indigenous People's Day / Thanksgiving Day (CA)	11
16	17 — Boss's Day	18 — Chocolate Cupcake Day
23	24 — Diwali	25

November

SUN	MON	TUE	WED	THU	FRI	SAT
			1	2	3	4	5
6	7	8	9	10	11	12
13	14	15	16	17	18	19
20	21	22	23	24	25	26
27	28	29	30			

If you want something said, ask a man;
if you want something done, ask a woman

- Margaret Thatcher

WEDNESDAY	THURSDAY	FRIDAY	SATURDAY
			01
05 Yom Kippur	06	07	08 The Prophet's Birthday
12	13	14	15
19	20	21	22
26	27	28	29

11

NOVEMBER
2022

October

SUN	MON	TUE	WED	THU	FRI	SAT
						1
2	3	4	5	6	7	8
9	10	11	12	13	14	15
16	17	18	19	20	21	22
23	24	25	26	27	28	29
30	31					

Major Goals

- [ ]
- [ ]
- [ ]
- [ ]
- [ ]
- [ ]
- [ ]
- [ ]

Notes

Important Dates

SUNDAY	MONDAY	TUESDAY
		01
06 Daylight Saving Time Ends	07	08 Election Day
13	14	15
20 Universal Children's Day	21	22
27 First Sunday of Advent	28	29

December

SUN	MON	TUE	WED	THU	FRI	SAT
					1	2	3
4	5	6	7	8	9	10
11	12	13	14	15	16	17
18	19	20	21	22	23	24
25	26	27	28	29	30	31

It is better to travel well than to arrive

- Buddha

WEDNESDAY	THURSDAY	FRIDAY	SATURDAY
02	03 Men Make Dinner Day	04	05
09	10	11 Veterans Day / Remembrance Day (CA)	12
16	17 Use Less Stuff Day	18	19
23	24 Thanksgiving Day	25 Black Friday	26
30			

12

DECEMBER

2022

November

SUN	MON	TUE	WED	THU	FRI	SAT
		1	2	3	4	5
6	7	8	9	10	11	12
13	14	15	16	17	18	19
20	21	22	23	24	25	26
27	28	29	30			

Major Goals

- ☐ _____
- ☐ _____
- ☐ _____
- ☐ _____
- ☐ _____
- ☐ _____
- ☐ _____
- ☐ _____

Notes

Important Dates

SUNDAY	MONDAY	TUESDAY
04	05 Day of the Ninja	06
11	12 Gingerbread House Day	13
18	19 Chanukah/Hanukkah (First day)	20
25 Christmas	26 Boxing Day (CA, UK) Kwanzaa Begins Christmas Observed	27

January

SUN	MON	TUE	WED	THU	FRI	SAT
1	2	3	4	5	6	7
8	9	10	11	12	13	14
15	16	17	18	19	20	21
22	23	24	25	26	27	28
29	30	31				

Simplicity is the keynote of all true elegance

- Coco Chanel

WEDNESDAY	THURSDAY	FRIDAY	SATURDAY
	01	02	03
07 Pearl Harbor Remembrance Day	08	09	10
14	15	16	17
21	22	23	24
28	29	30	31 New Year's Eve

Notes

Notes

2023 Calendar

January

SUN	MON	TUE	WED	THU	FRI	SAT
1	2	3	4	5	6	7
8	9	10	11	12	13	14
15	16	17	18	19	20	21
22	23	24	25	26	27	28
29	30	31				

February

SUN	MON	TUE	WED	THU	FRI	SAT
			1	2	3	4
5	6	7	8	9	10	11
12	13	14	15	16	17	18
19	20	21	22	23	24	25
26	27	28				

March

SUN	MON	TUE	WED	THU	FRI	SAT
			1	2	3	4
5	6	7	8	9	10	11
12	13	14	15	16	17	18
19	20	21	22	23	24	25
26	27	28	29	30	31	

April

SUN	MON	TUE	WED	THU	FRI	SAT
						1
2	3	4	5	6	7	8
9	10	11	12	13	14	15
16	17	18	19	20	21	22
23	24	25	26	27	28	29
30						

May

SUN	MON	TUE	WED	THU	FRI	SAT
	1	2	3	4	5	6
7	8	9	10	11	12	13
14	15	16	17	18	19	20
21	22	23	24	25	26	27
28	29	30	31			

June

SUN	MON	TUE	WED	THU	FRI	SAT
				1	2	3
4	5	6	7	8	9	10
11	12	13	14	15	16	17
18	19	20	21	22	23	24
25	26	27	28	29	30	

July

SUN	MON	TUE	WED	THU	FRI	SAT
						1
2	3	4	5	6	7	8
9	10	11	12	13	14	15
16	17	18	19	20	21	22
23	24	25	26	27	28	29
30	31					

August

SUN	MON	TUE	WED	THU	FRI	SAT
		1	2	3	4	5
6	7	8	9	10	11	12
13	14	15	16	17	18	19
20	21	22	23	24	25	26
27	28	29	30	31		

September

SUN	MON	TUE	WED	THU	FRI	SAT
					1	2
3	4	5	6	7	8	9
10	11	12	13	14	15	16
17	18	19	20	21	22	23
24	25	26	27	28	29	30

October

SUN	MON	TUE	WED	THU	FRI	SAT
1	2	3	4	5	6	7
8	9	10	11	12	13	14
15	16	17	18	19	20	21
22	23	24	25	26	27	28
29	30	31				

November

SUN	MON	TUE	WED	THU	FRI	SAT
		1	2	3	4	
5	6	7	8	9	10	11
12	13	14	15	16	17	18
19	20	21	22	23	24	25
26	27	28	29	30		

December

SUN	MON	TUE	WED	THU	FRI	SAT
					1	2
3	4	5	6	7	8	9
10	11	12	13	14	15	16
17	18	19	20	21	22	23
24	25	26	27	28	29	30
31						

2023 *Holidays*

This planner features US and Canada (CA) legal holidays, important observances of major world religions and some fun days as well. *The holidays listed in this planner are accurate to be best of our knowledge and research.*

JANUARY

1   New Year's Day
5   National Keto Day
16 Martin Luther King Jr. Day
19 National Popcorn Day
22 Chinese New Year

FEBRUARY

2   Groundhog Day
4   Eat Ice Cream for Breakfast Day
5   Super Bowl
14 Valentine's Day
15 National Flag of Canada Day
20 Presidents' Day
21 Mardi Gras
22 Ash Wednesday, Lent Begins

MARCH

8   International Women's Day, Holi
12 Daylight Saving Time Started
17 St. Patrick's Day
23 First Day of Ramadan
    Puppy Day

APRIL

1   April Fool's Day
6   Passover (First day)
7   Good Friday
9   Easter Sunday
10 Easter Monday (CA)
20 Look Alike Day
22 Earth Day, Eid al-Fitr

MAY

1   May Day
5   Cinco de Mayo
6   National Nurses Day
14 Mother's Day
20 Armed Forces Day
    Be a Millionaire Day
22 Victoria Day (CA)
26 Shavuot
29 Memorial Day

JUNE

5   World Environment Day
6   D-Day
8   Best Friends Day
14 Flag Day
18 Father's Day
19 Juneteenth
24 Swim a Lap Day
29 Eid al-Adha

JULY

1   Canada Day
3   International Plastic Bag Free Day
4   Independence Day
16 Ice Cream Day
19 Muharram
23 Parents' Day
30 National Cheesecake Day

AUGUST

6   Sisters' Day
7   Civic Holiday (CA)
    Purple Heart Day (observance only)
16 Tell a Joke Day
26 Women's Equality Day

SEPTEMBER

4   Labor Day (USA, CA)
5   Cheese Pizza Day
10 National Grandparents Day
11 Patriot Day
16 Rosh Hashana
25 Yom Kippur, Comic Book Day
27 The Prophet's Birthday
30 First Day of Sukkot

OCTOBER

4   Taco Day
9   Columbus Day
    Indigenous People's Day
    Thanksgiving Day (CA)
16 Boss's Day
18 Chocolate Cupcake Day
31 Halloween

NOVEMBER

2   Men Make Dinner Day
5   Daylight Saving Time Ends
7   Election Day
9   Diwali
10 Veterans Day observed
11 Remembrance Day (CA)
16 Use Less Stuff Day
20 Universal Children's Day
23 Thanksgiving Day
24 Black Friday

DECEMBER

3   First Sunday of Advent
5   Day of the Ninja
7   Pearl Harbor Remembrance Day
8   Chanukah/Hanukkah (First day)
12 Gingerbread House Day
25 Christmas
26 Kwanzaa Begins, Boxing Day (CA, UK)
31 New Year's Eve

01

JANUARY
2023

December

SUN	MON	TUE	WED	THU	FRI	SAT
				1	2	3
4	5	6	7	8	9	10
11	12	13	14	15	16	17
18	19	20	21	22	23	24
25	26	27	28	29	30	31

Major Goals

- [ ] _____
- [ ] _____
- [ ] _____
- [ ] _____
- [ ] _____
- [ ] _____
- [ ] _____
- [ ] _____

Notes

Important Dates

SUNDAY	MONDAY	TUESDAY
01 — New Year's Day	02	03
08	09	10
15	16 — Martin Luther King Jr. Day	17
22 — Chinese New Year	23	24
29	30	31

February

SUN	MON	TUE	WED	THU	FRI	SAT
			1	2	3	4
5	6	7	8	9	10	11
12	13	14	15	16	17	18
19	20	21	22	23	24	25
26	27	28				

Be happy for this moment. This moment in your life

\- Omar Khayyam

WEDNESDAY	THURSDAY	FRIDAY	SATURDAY
04	05 National Keto Day	06	07
11	12	13	14
18	19 National Popcorn Day	20	21
25	26	27	28

02

FEBRUARY
2023

January

SUN	MON	TUE	WED	THU	FRI	SAT
1	2	3	4	5	6	7
8	9	10	11	12	13	14
15	16	17	18	19	20	21
22	23	24	25	26	27	28
29	30	31				

Major Goals

- [ ] _____
- [ ] _____
- [ ] _____
- [ ] _____
- [ ] _____
- [ ] _____
- [ ] _____
- [ ] _____

Notes

Important Dates

SUNDAY	MONDAY	TUESDAY
05 Super Bowl	06	07
12	13	14 Valentine's Day
19	20 Presidents' Day	21 Mardi Gras
26	27	28

March

SUN	MON	TUE	WED	THU	FRI	SAT
			1	2	3	4
5	6	7	8	9	10	11
12	13	14	15	16	17	18
19	20	21	22	23	24	25
26	27	28	29	30	31	

Nothing can dim the light that shines from within

- Maya Angelou

WEDNESDAY	THURSDAY	FRIDAY	SATURDAY
01	02 Groundhog Day	03	04 Eat Ice Cream for Breakfast Day
08	09	10	11
15 National Flag of Canada Day	16	17	18
22 Ash Wednesday, Lent Begins	23	24	25

03

MARCH
2023

February

SUN	MON	TUE	WED	THU	FRI	SAT
			1	2	3	4
5	6	7	8	9	10	11
12	13	14	15	16	17	18
19	20	21	22	23	24	25
26	27	28				

Major Goals

- ☐ _____
- ☐ _____
- ☐ _____
- ☐ _____
- ☐ _____
- ☐ _____
- ☐ _____
- ☐ _____

Notes

Important Dates

SUNDAY	MONDAY	TUESDAY
05	06	07
12 Daylight Saving Time Started	13	14
19	20	21
26	27	28

April

SUN	MON	TUE	WED	THU	FRI	SAT
						1
2	3	4	5	6	7	8
9	10	11	12	13	14	15
16	17	18	19	20	21	22
23	24	25	26	27	28	29
30						

A friend is like a four leaf clover, hard to find and lucky to have

- Irish Proverb

WEDNESDAY	THURSDAY	FRIDAY	SATURDAY
01	02	03	04
08 International Women's Day Holi	09	10	11
15	16	17 St. Patrick's Day	18
22	23 First Day of Ramadan Puppy Day	24	25
29	30	31	

04

APRIL
2023

March

SUN	MON	TUE	WED	THU	FRI	SAT
			1	2	3	4
5	6	7	8	9	10	11
12	13	14	15	16	17	18
19	20	21	22	23	24	25
26	27	28	29	30	31	

Major Goals

- ☐
- ☐
- ☐
- ☐
- ☐
- ☐
- ☐
- ☐

Notes

Important Dates

SUNDAY	MONDAY	TUESDAY
30		
02	03	04
09 Easter Sunday	10 Easter Monday (CA)	11
16	17	18
23	24	25

May

SUN	MON	TUE	WED	THU	FRI	SAT
	1	2	3	4	5	6
7	8	9	10	11	12	13
14	15	16	17	18	19	20
21	22	23	24	25	26	27
28	29	30	31			

Despite the forecast, live like it's spring

- Lily Pulitzer

WEDNESDAY	THURSDAY	FRIDAY	SATURDAY
			01 April Fool's Day
05	06 Passover (First day)	07 Good Friday	08
12	13	14	15
19	20 Look Alike Day	21	22 Earth Day / Eid al-Fitr
26	27	28	29

05

MAY
2023

April

SUN	MON	TUE	WED	THU	FRI	SAT
						1
2	3	4	5	6	7	8
9	10	11	12	13	14	15
16	17	18	19	20	21	22
23	24	25	26	27	28	29
30						

Major Goals

- ☐ _____
- ☐ _____
- ☐ _____
- ☐ _____
- ☐ _____
- ☐ _____
- ☐ _____
- ☐ _____

Notes

Important Dates

SUNDAY	MONDAY	TUESDAY
	01 May Day	02
07	08	09
14 Mother's Day	15	16
21	22 Victoria Day (CA)	23
28	29 Memorial Day	30

June

SUN	MON	TUE	WED	THU	FRI	SAT
				1	2	3
4	5	6	7	8	9	10
11	12	13	14	15	16	17
18	19	20	21	22	23	24
25	26	27	28	29	30	

All progress takes place outside the comfort zone

- Michael John Bobak

WEDNESDAY	THURSDAY	FRIDAY	SATURDAY
03	04	05 Cinco de Mayo	06 National Nurses Day
10	11	12	13
17	18	19	20 Armed Forces Day / Be a Millionaire Day
24	25	26 Shavuot	27
31			

06

JUNE
2023

May

SUN	MON	TUE	WED	THU	FRI	SAT
	1	2	3	4	5	6
7	8	9	10	11	12	13
14	15	16	17	18	19	20
21	22	23	24	25	26	27
28	29	30	31			

Major Goals

- [ ] _____
- [ ] _____
- [ ] _____
- [ ] _____
- [ ] _____
- [ ] _____
- [ ] _____
- [ ] _____

Notes

Important Dates

SUNDAY	MONDAY	TUESDAY
04	05 World Environment Day	06 D-Day
11	12	13
18 Father's Day	19 Juneteenth	20
25	26	27

July

SUN	MON	TUE	WED	THU	FRI	SAT
						1
2	3	4	5	6	7	8
9	10	11	12	13	14	15
16	17	18	19	20	21	22
23	24	25	26	27	28	29
30	31					

You don't have to play masculine to be a strong woman

– Mary Elizabeth Winstead

WEDNESDAY	THURSDAY	FRIDAY	SATURDAY
	01	02	03
07	08 Best Friends Day	09	10
14 Flag Day	15	16	17
21	22	23	24 Swim a Lap Day
28	29 Eid al-Adha	30	

07

JULY

2023

June

SUN	MON	TUE	WED	THU	FRI	SAT
				1	2	3
4	5	6	7	8	9	10
11	12	13	14	15	16	17
18	19	20	21	22	23	24
25	26	27	28	29	30	

Major Goals

- ☐ _____
- ☐ _____
- ☐ _____
- ☐ _____
- ☐ _____
- ☐ _____
- ☐ _____
- ☐ _____

Notes

Important Dates

SUNDAY	MONDAY	TUESDAY
30 National Cheesecake Day	**31**	
02	**03** International Plastic Bag Free Day	**04** Independence Day
09	**10**	**11**
16 Ice Cream Day	**17**	**18**
23 Parents' Day	**24**	**25**

August

SUN	MON	TUE	WED	THU	FRI	SAT
		1	2	3	4	5
6	7	8	9	10	11	12
13	14	15	16	17	18	19
20	21	22	23	24	25	26
27	28	29	30	31		

Nothing is impossible. The word itself says , 'i'm possible!

- Audrey Hepburn

WEDNESDAY	THURSDAY	FRIDAY	SATURDAY
			01 Canada Day
05	06	07	08
12	13	14	15
19 Muharram	20	21	22
26	27	28	29

08

AUGUST
2023

July
SUN	MON	TUE	WED	THU	FRI	SAT
						1
2	3	4	5	6	7	8
9	10	11	12	13	14	15
16	17	18	19	20	21	22
23	24	25	26	27	28	29
30	31					

Major Goals

- ☐ _____
- ☐ _____
- ☐ _____
- ☐ _____
- ☐ _____
- ☐ _____
- ☐ _____
- ☐ _____

Notes

Important Dates

SUNDAY	MONDAY	TUESDAY
		01
06 Sisters' Day	07 Civic Holiday (CA) Purple Heart Day (observance only)	08
13	14	15
20	21	22
27	28	29

September

SUN	MON	TUE	WED	THU	FRI	SAT
					1	2
3	4	5	6	7	8	9
10	11	12	13	14	15	16
17	18	19	20	21	22	23
24	25	26	27	28	29	30

Wherever you go, go with all your heart

- Confucius

WEDNESDAY	THURSDAY	FRIDAY	SATURDAY
02	03	04	05
09	10	11	12
16 Tell a Joke Day	17	18	19
23	24	25	26 Women's Equality Day
30	31		

09

SEPTEMBER
2023

August

SUN	MON	TUE	WED	THU	FRI	SAT
		1	2	3	4	5
6	7	8	9	10	11	12
13	14	15	16	17	18	19
20	21	22	23	24	25	26
27	28	29	30	31		

Major Goals

- ☐ _____
- ☐ _____
- ☐ _____
- ☐ _____
- ☐ _____
- ☐ _____
- ☐ _____
- ☐ _____

Notes

Important Dates

SUNDAY	MONDAY	TUESDAY
03	04 Labor Day (USA, CA)	05 Cheese Pizza Day
10 National Grandparents Day	11 Patriot Day	12
17	18	19
24	25 Yom Kippur / Comic Book Day	26

October

SUN	MON	TUE	WED	THU	FRI	SAT
1	2	3	4	5	6	7
8	9	10	11	12	13	14
15	16	17	18	19	20	21
22	23	24	25	26	27	28
29	30	31				

Work is always an antidote to depression

- Eleanor Roosevelt

WEDNESDAY	THURSDAY	FRIDAY	SATURDAY
		01	02
06	07	08	09
13	14	15	16 Rosh Hashana
20	21	22	23
27 The Prophet's Birthday	28	29	30 First Day of Sukkot

10 OCTOBER
2023

September

SUN	MON	TUE	WED	THU	FRI	SAT
					1	2
3	4	5	6	7	8	9
10	11	12	13	14	15	16
17	18	19	20	21	22	23
24	25	26	27	28	29	30

Major Goals

- [ ] _____
- [ ] _____
- [ ] _____
- [ ] _____
- [ ] _____
- [ ] _____
- [ ] _____
- [ ] _____

Notes

Important Dates

SUNDAY	MONDAY	TUESDAY
01	02	03
08	09 Columbus Day / Indigenous People's Day / Thanksgiving Day (CA)	10
15	16 Boss's Day	17
22	23	24
29	30	31 Halloween

November

SUN	MON	TUE	WED	THU	FRI	SAT
			1	2	3	4
5	6	7	8	9	10	11
12	13	14	15	16	17	18
19	20	21	22	23	24	25
26	27	28	29	30		

You will learn by reading, but you will understand with love

- Rumi

WEDNESDAY	THURSDAY	FRIDAY	SATURDAY
04 Taco Day	05	06	07
11	12	13	14
18 Chocolate Cupcake Day	19	20	21
25	26	27	28

11

NOVEMBER
2023

October

SUN	MON	TUE	WED	THU	FRI	SAT
1	2	3	4	5	6	7
8	9	10	11	12	13	14
15	16	17	18	19	20	21
22	23	24	25	26	27	28
29	30	31				

Major Goals

- ☐ _____
- ☐ _____
- ☐ _____
- ☐ _____
- ☐ _____
- ☐ _____
- ☐ _____
- ☐ _____

Notes

Important Dates

SUNDAY	MONDAY	TUESDAY
05 Daylight Saving Time Ends	06	07 Election Day
12	13	14
19	20 Universal Children's Day	21
26	27	28

December

SUN	MON	TUE	WED	THU	FRI	SAT
					1	2
3	4	5	6	7	8	9
10	11	12	13	14	15	16
17	18	19	20	21	22	23
24	25	26	27	28	29	30
31						

Laziness may appear attractive, but work gives satisfaction

- Anne Frank

WEDNESDAY	THURSDAY	FRIDAY	SATURDAY
01	02 Men Make Dinner Day	03	04
08	09 Diwali	10 Veterans Day observed	11 Remembrance Day (CA)
15	16 Use Less Stuff Day	17	18
22	23 Thanksgiving Day	24 Black Friday	25
29	30		

12

DECEMBER
2023

November

SUN	MON	TUE	WED	THU	FRI	SAT
			1	2	3	4
5	6	7	8	9	10	11
12	13	14	15	16	17	18
19	20	21	22	23	24	25
26	27	28	29	30		

Major Goals

- ☐ _____
- ☐ _____
- ☐ _____
- ☐ _____
- ☐ _____
- ☐ _____
- ☐ _____
- ☐ _____

Notes

Important Dates

SUNDAY	MONDAY	TUESDAY
31 New Year's Eve		
03 First Sunday of Advent	**04**	**05** Day of the Ninja
10	**11**	**12** Gingerbread House Day
17	**18**	**19**
24	**25** Christmas	**26** Kwanzaa Begins Boxing Day (CA, UK)

January

SUN	MON	TUE	WED	THU	FRI	SAT
	1	2	3	4	5	6
7	8	9	10	11	12	13
14	15	16	17	18	19	20
21	22	23	24	25	26	27
28	29	30	31			

Do all things with love

- OgMandino

WEDNESDAY	THURSDAY	FRIDAY	SATURDAY
		01	02
06	07 Pearl Harbor Remembrance Day	08 Chanukah/Hanukkah (First day)	09
13	14	15	16
20	21	22	23
27	28	29	30

Notes

Notes

2024 Calendar

January

SUN	MON	TUE	WED	THU	FRI	SAT
	1	2	3	4	5	6
7	8	9	10	11	12	13
14	15	16	17	18	19	20
21	22	23	24	25	26	27
28	29	30	31			

February

SUN	MON	TUE	WED	THU	FRI	SAT
				1	2	3
4	5	6	7	8	9	10
11	12	13	14	15	16	17
18	19	20	21	22	23	24
25	26	27	28	29		

March

SUN	MON	TUE	WED	THU	FRI	SAT
					1	2
3	4	5	6	7	8	9
10	11	12	13	14	15	16
17	18	19	20	21	22	23
24	25	26	27	28	29	30
31						

April

SUN	MON	TUE	WED	THU	FRI	SAT
	1	2	3	4	5	6
7	8	9	10	11	12	13
14	15	16	17	18	19	20
21	22	23	24	25	26	27
28	29	30				

May

SUN	MON	TUE	WED	THU	FRI	SAT
			1	2	3	4
5	6	7	8	9	10	11
12	13	14	15	16	17	18
19	20	21	22	23	24	25
26	27	28	29	30	31	

June

SUN	MON	TUE	WED	THU	FRI	SAT
						1
2	3	4	5	6	7	8
9	10	11	12	13	14	15
16	17	18	19	20	21	22
23	24	25	26	27	28	29
30						

July

SUN	MON	TUE	WED	THU	FRI	SAT
	1	2	3	4	5	6
7	8	9	10	11	12	13
14	15	16	17	18	19	20
21	22	23	24	25	26	27
28	29	30	31			

August

SUN	MON	TUE	WED	THU	FRI	SAT
				1	2	3
4	5	6	7	8	9	10
11	12	13	14	15	16	17
18	19	20	21	22	23	24
25	26	27	28	29	30	31

September

SUN	MON	TUE	WED	THU	FRI	SAT
1	2	3	4	5	6	7
8	9	10	11	12	13	14
15	16	17	18	19	20	21
22	23	24	25	26	27	28
29	30					

October

SUN	MON	TUE	WED	THU	FRI	SAT
		1	2	3	4	5
6	7	8	9	10	11	12
13	14	15	16	17	18	19
20	21	22	23	24	25	26
27	28	29	30	31		

November

SUN	MON	TUE	WED	THU	FRI	SAT
					1	2
3	4	5	6	7	8	9
10	11	12	13	14	15	16
17	18	19	20	21	22	23
24	25	26	27	28	29	30

December

SUN	MON	TUE	WED	THU	FRI	SAT
1	2	3	4	5	6	7
8	9	10	11	12	13	14
15	16	17	18	19	20	21
22	23	24	25	26	27	28
29	30	31				

2024 *Holidays*

This planner features US and Canada (CA) legal holidays, important observances of major world religions and some fun days as well. *The holidays listed in this planner are accurate to be best of our knowledge and research.*

JANUARY

1   New Year's Day
5   National Keto Day
15 Martin Luther King Jr. Day
19 National Popcorn Day

FEBRUARY

2   Groundhog Day
3   Eat Ice Cream for Breakfast Day
4   Super Bowl
10 Chinese New Year
13 Mardi Gras
14 Valentine's Day
    Ash Wednesday
    Lent Begins
15 National Flag of Canada Day
19 Presidents' Day

MARCH

8   International Women's Day
10 Daylight Saving Time Started
11 First Day of Ramadan
17 St. Patrick's Day
23 Puppy Day
26 Holi
29 Good Friday
31 Easter Sunday

APRIL

1   Easter Monday (CA)
    April Fool's Day
10 Eid al-Fitr
20 Look Alike Day
22 Earth Day
23 Passover (First day)

MAY

1   May Day
5   Cinco de Mayo
6   National Nurses Day
12 Mother's Day
18 Armed Forces Day
20 Victoria Day (CA)
    Be a Millionaire Day
27 Memorial Day

JUNE

5   World Environment Day
6   D-Day
8   Best Friends Day
12 Shavuot
14 Flag Day
16 Father's Day
17 Eid al-Adha
19 Juneteenth
24 Swim a Lap Day

JULY

1   Canada Day
3   International Plastic Bag Free Day
4   Independence Day
8   Muharram
21 Ice Cream Day
28 Parents' Day
30 National Cheesecake Day

AUGUST

4   Sisters' Day
5   Civic Holiday (CA)
7   Purple Heart Day
16 Tell a Joke Day
26 Women's Equality Day

SEPTEMBER

2   Labor Day (USA, CA)
5   Cheese Pizza Day
8   National Grandparents Day
11 Patriot Day
16 The Prophet's Birthday
25 Comic Book Day

OCTOBER

3   Rosh Hashana
4   Taco Day
12 Yom Kippur
14 Columbus Day
    Indigenous People's Day
    Thanksgiving Day (CA)
16 Boss's Day
17 First Day of Sukkot
18 Chocolate Cupcake Day
31 Halloween

NOVEMBER

1   Diwali
3   Daylight Saving Time Ends
5   Election Day
7   Men Make Dinner Day
11 Veterans Day, Remembrance Day (CA)
20 Universal Children's Day
21 Use Less Stuff Day
28 Thanksgiving Day
29 Black Friday

DECEMBER

1   First Sunday of Advent
5   Day of the Ninja
7   Pearl Harbor Remembrance Day
12 Gingerbread House Day
25 Christmas
26 Chanukah/Hanukkah (First day)
    Kwanzaa Begins
    Boxing Day (CA, UK)
31 New Year's Eve

01

JANUARY
2024

December

SUN	MON	TUE	WED	THU	FRI	SAT
					1	2
3	4	5	6	7	8	9
10	11	12	13	14	15	16
17	18	19	20	21	22	23
24	25	26	27	28	29	30
31						

Major Goals

- [ ] _____
- [ ] _____
- [ ] _____
- [ ] _____
- [ ] _____
- [ ] _____
- [ ] _____
- [ ] _____

Notes

Important Dates

SUNDAY	MONDAY	TUESDAY
	01 New Year's Day	02
07	08	09
14	15 Martin Luther King Jr. Day	16
21	22	23
28	29	30

February

SUN	MON	TUE	WED	THU	FRI	SAT
				1	2	3
4	5	6	7	8	9	10
11	12	13	14	15	16	17
18	19	20	21	22	23	24
25	26	27	28	29		

The only safe ship in a storm is leadership

- Faye Wattleton

WEDNESDAY	THURSDAY	FRIDAY	SATURDAY
03	04	05 National Keto Day	06
10	11	12	13
17	18	19 National Popcorn Day	20
24	25	26	27
31			

02

FEBRUARY
2024

January

SUN	MON	TUE	WED	THU	FRI	SAT
	1	2	3	4	5	6
7	8	9	10	11	12	13
14	15	16	17	18	19	20
21	22	23	24	25	26	27
28	29	30	31			

Major Goals

- ☐ _____
- ☐ _____
- ☐ _____
- ☐ _____
- ☐ _____
- ☐ _____
- ☐ _____
- ☐ _____

Notes

Important Dates

SUNDAY	MONDAY	TUESDAY
04 Super Bowl	05	06
11	12	13 Mardi Gras
18	19 Presidents' Day 20	
25	26	27

March

SUN	MON	TUE	WED	THU	FRI	SAT
					1	2
3	4	5	6	7	8	9
10	11	12	13	14	15	16
17	18	19	20	21	22	23
24	25	26	27	28	29	30
31						

The fastest way to change society is to mobilize the women of the world

– Charles Malik

WEDNESDAY	THURSDAY	FRIDAY	SATURDAY
	01	02 Groundhog Day	03 Eat Ice Cream for Breakfast Day
07	08	09	10 Chinese New Year
14 Valentine's Day Ash Wednesday Lent Begins	15 National Flag of Canada Day	16	17
21	22	23	24
28	29		

03

MARCH
2024

February

SUN	MON	TUE	WED	THU	FRI	SAT
				1	2	3
4	5	6	7	8	9	10
11	12	13	14	15	16	17
18	19	20	21	22	23	24
25	26	27	28	29		

Major Goals

- ☐ _____
- ☐ _____
- ☐ _____
- ☐ _____
- ☐ _____
- ☐ _____
- ☐ _____
- ☐ _____

Notes

Important Dates

SUNDAY	MONDAY	TUESDAY
31 Easter Sunday		
03	**04**	**05**
10 Daylight Saving Time Started	**11** First Day of Ramadan	**12**
17 St. Patrick's Day	**18**	**19**
24	**25**	**26** Holi

April

SUN	MON	TUE	WED	THU	FRI	SAT
		1	2	3	4	5	6
7	8	9	10	11	12	13
14	15	16	17	18	19	20
21	22	23	24	25	26	27
28	29	30				

There is nothing permanent except change

- Heraclitus

WEDNESDAY	THURSDAY	FRIDAY	SATURDAY
		01	02
06	07	08 International Women's Day	09
13	14	15	16
20	21	22	23 Puppy Day
27	28	29 Good Friday	30

04

APRIL
2024

March

SUN	MON	TUE	WED	THU	FRI	SAT
					1	2
3	4	5	6	7	8	9
10	11	12	13	14	15	16
17	18	19	20	21	22	23
24	25	26	27	28	29	30
31						

Major Goals

- ☐ _____
- ☐ _____
- ☐ _____
- ☐ _____
- ☐ _____
- ☐ _____
- ☐ _____
- ☐ _____

Notes

Important Dates

SUNDAY	MONDAY	TUESDAY
	01 — Easter Monday (CA) / April Fool's Day	02
07	08	09
14	15	16
21	22 — Earth Day	23 — Passover (First day)
28	29	30

May

SUN	MON	TUE	WED	THU	FRI	SAT
			1	2	3	4
5	6	7	8	9	10	11
12	13	14	15	16	17	18
19	20	21	22	23	24	25
26	27	28	29	30	31	

When you lose a couple of times
It makes you realize how difficult it is to win

\- Steffi Graf

WEDNESDAY	THURSDAY	FRIDAY	SATURDAY
03	04	05	06
10 Eid al-Fitr	11	12	13
17	18	19	20 Look Alike Day
24	25	26	27

05

MAY
2024

April

SUN	MON	TUE	WED	THU	FRI	SAT
	1	2	3	4	5	6
7	8	9	10	11	12	13
14	15	16	17	18	19	20
21	22	23	24	25	26	27
28	29	30				

Major Goals

- [ ]
- [ ]
- [ ]
- [ ]
- [ ]
- [ ]
- [ ]
- [ ]

Notes

Important Dates

SUNDAY	MONDAY	TUESDAY
05 Cinco de Mayo	06 National Nurses Day	07
12 Mother's Day	13	14
19	20 Victoria Day (CA) Be a Millionaire Day	21
26	27 Memorial Day	28

June

The secret of getting ahead is getting started

\- Mark Twain

WEDNESDAY	THURSDAY	FRIDAY	SATURDAY
01 May Day	02	03	04
08	09	10	11
15	16	17	18 Armed Forces Day
22	23	24	25
29	30	31	

06

JUNE
2024

May

SUN	MON	TUE	WED	THU	FRI	SAT
			1	2	3	4
5	6	7	8	9	10	11
12	13	14	15	16	17	18
19	20	21	22	23	24	25
26	27	28	29	30	31	

Major Goals

- [ ]
- [ ]
- [ ]
- [ ]
- [ ]
- [ ]
- [ ]
- [ ]

Notes

Important Dates

SUNDAY	MONDAY	TUESDAY
30		
02	03	04
09	10	11
16 Father's Day	17 Eid al-Adha	18
23	24 Swim a Lap Day	25

July

SUN	MON	TUE	WED	THU	FRI	SAT
		1	2	3	4	5	6
7	8	9	10	11	12	13
14	15	16	17	18	19	20
21	22	23	24	25	26	27
28	29	30	31			

Above all, be the heroine of your life, not the victim

- Nora Ephron

WEDNESDAY	THURSDAY	FRIDAY	SATURDAY
			01
05 World Environment Day	06 D-Day	07	08 Best Friends Day
12 Shavuot	13	14 Flag Day	15
19 Juneteenth	20	21	22
26	27	28	29

07

JULY
2024

June

SUN	MON	TUE	WED	THU	FRI	SAT
						1
2	3	4	5	6	7	8
9	10	11	12	13	14	15
16	17	18	19	20	21	22
23	24	25	26	27	28	29
30						

Major Goals

☐ _____
☐ _____
☐ _____
☐ _____
☐ _____
☐ _____
☐ _____
☐ _____

Notes

Important Dates

SUNDAY	MONDAY	TUESDAY
	01 Canada Day	02
07	08 Muharram	09
14	15	16
21 Ice Cream Day	22	23
28 Parents' Day	29	30 National Cheesecake Day

August

SUN	MON	TUE	WED	THU	FRI	SAT
					1	2	3
4	5	6	7	8	9	10
11	12	13	14	15	16	17
18	19	20	21	22	23	24
25	26	27	28	29	30	31

Innovation distinguishes between a leader and a follower

- Steve Jobs

WEDNESDAY	THURSDAY	FRIDAY	SATURDAY
03 International Plastic Bag Free Day	04 Independence Day	05	06
10	11	12	13
17	18	19	20
24	25	26	27
31			

08

AUGUST
2024

July
SUN	MON	TUE	WED	THU	FRI	SAT
	1	2	3	4	5	6
7	8	9	10	11	12	13
14	15	16	17	18	19	20
21	22	23	24	25	26	27
28	29	30	31			

Major Goals

- ☐ _____
- ☐ _____
- ☐ _____
- ☐ _____
- ☐ _____
- ☐ _____
- ☐ _____
- ☐ _____

Notes

Important Dates

SUNDAY	MONDAY	TUESDAY
04 Sisters' Day	05 Civic Holiday (CA)	06
11	12	13
18	19	20
25	26 Women's Equality Day	27

September

SUN	MON	TUE	WED	THU	FRI	SAT
1	2	3	4	5	6	7
8	9	10	11	12	13	14
15	16	17	18	19	20	21
22	23	24	25	26	27	28
29	30					

With the new day comes new strength and new thoughts

– Eleanor Roosevelt

WEDNESDAY	THURSDAY	FRIDAY	SATURDAY
	01	02	03
07 Purple Heart Day	08	09	10
14	15	16 Tell a Joke Day	17
21	22	23	24
28	29	30	31

09

SEPTEMBER
2024

August

SUN	MON	TUE	WED	THU	FRI	SAT
				1	2	3
4	5	6	7	8	9	10
11	12	13	14	15	16	17
18	19	20	21	22	23	24
25	26	27	28	29	30	31

Major Goals

- ☐ _____
- ☐ _____
- ☐ _____
- ☐ _____
- ☐ _____
- ☐ _____
- ☐ _____
- ☐ _____

Notes

Important Dates

SUNDAY	MONDAY	TUESDAY
01	02 Labor Day (USA, CA)	03
08 National Grandparents Day	09	10
15	16 The Prophet's Birthday	17
22	23	24
29	30	

October

SUN	MON	TUE	WED	THU	FRI	SAT
		1	2	3	4	5
6	7	8	9	10	11	12
13	14	15	16	17	18	19
20	21	22	23	24	25	26
27	28	29	30	31		

Wherever you are, and whatever you do, be in love

\- Rumi

WEDNESDAY	THURSDAY	FRIDAY	SATURDAY
04	05 Cheese Pizza Day	06	07
11 Patriot Day	12	13	14
18	19	20	21
25 Comic Book Day	26	27	28

10

OCTOBER
2024

September

SUN	MON	TUE	WED	THU	FRI	SAT
1	2	3	4	5	6	7
8	9	10	11	12	13	14
15	16	17	18	19	20	21
22	23	24	25	26	27	28
29	30					

Major Goals

- ☐ _____
- ☐ _____
- ☐ _____
- ☐ _____
- ☐ _____
- ☐ _____
- ☐ _____
- ☐ _____

Notes

Important Dates

SUNDAY	MONDAY	TUESDAY
		01
06	07	08
13	14	Columbus Day Indigenous People's Day Thanksgiving Day (CA) 15
20	21	22
27	28	29

November

SUN	MON	TUE	WED	THU	FRI	SAT
					1	2
3	4	5	6	7	8	9
10	11	12	13	14	15	16
17	18	19	20	21	22	23
24	25	26	27	28	29	30

Kindness is always fashionable, and always welcome

– Amelia Barr

WEDNESDAY	THURSDAY	FRIDAY	SATURDAY
02	03 Rosh Hashana	04 Taco Day	05
09	10	11	12 Yom Kippur
16 Boss's Day	17 First Day of Sukkot	18 Chocolate Cupcake Day	19
23	24	25	26
30	31 Halloween		

11

NOVEMBER
2024

October

SUN	MON	TUE	WED	THU	FRI	SAT
		1	2	3	4	5
6	7	8	9	10	11	12
13	14	15	16	17	18	19
20	21	22	23	24	25	26
27	28	29	30	31		

Major Goals

- ☐ _____
- ☐ _____
- ☐ _____
- ☐ _____
- ☐ _____
- ☐ _____
- ☐ _____
- ☐ _____

Notes

Important Dates

SUNDAY	MONDAY	TUESDAY
03 Daylight Saving Time Ends	04	05 Election Day
10	11 Veterans Day Remembrance Day (CA)	12
17	18	19
24	25	26

December

SUN	MON	TUE	WED	THU	FRI	SAT
1	2	3	4	5	6	7
8	9	10	11	12	13	14
15	16	17	18	19	20	21
22	23	24	25	26	27	28
29	30	31				

The way to get started is to quit talking and begin doing

- Walt Disney

WEDNESDAY	THURSDAY	FRIDAY	SATURDAY
		01 Diwali	02
06	07 Men Make Dinner Day	08	09
13	14	15	16
20 Universal Children's Day	21 Use Less Stuff Day	22	23
27	28 Thanksgiving Day	29 Black Friday	30

12 DECEMBER
2024

November

SUN	MON	TUE	WED	THU	FRI	SAT
					1	2
3	4	5	6	7	8	9
10	11	12	13	14	15	16
17	18	19	20	21	22	23
24	25	26	27	28	29	30

Major Goals

- ☐ _____
- ☐ _____
- ☐ _____
- ☐ _____
- ☐ _____
- ☐ _____
- ☐ _____
- ☐ _____

Notes

Important Dates

SUNDAY	MONDAY	TUESDAY
01 First Sunday of Advent	02	03
08	09	10
15	16	17
22	23	24
29	30	31 New Year's Eve

January

SUN	MON	TUE	WED	THU	FRI	SAT
				1	2	3	4
5	6	7	8	9	10	11
12	13	14	15	16	17	18
19	20	21	22	23	24	25
26	27	28	29	30	31	

Hard work has made it easy. That is my secret. That is why i win

- Nadia Comaneci

WEDNESDAY	THURSDAY	FRIDAY	SATURDAY
04	05 Day of the Ninja	06	07 Pearl Harbor Remembrance Day
11	12 Gingerbread House Day	13	14
18	19	20	21
25 Christmas	26 Chanukah/Hanukkah (First day) Kwanzaa Begins Boxing Day (CA, UK)	27	28

Notes

Notes

2025 Calendar

January

SUN	MON	TUE	WED	THU	FRI	SAT
			1	2	3	4
5	6	7	8	9	10	11
12	13	14	15	16	17	18
19	20	21	22	23	24	25
26	27	28	29	30	31	

February

SUN	MON	TUE	WED	THU	FRI	SAT
						1
2	3	4	5	6	7	8
9	10	11	12	13	14	15
16	17	18	19	20	21	22
23	24	25	26	27	28	

March

SUN	MON	TUE	WED	THU	FRI	SAT
						1
2	3	4	5	6	7	8
9	10	11	12	13	14	15
16	17	18	19	20	21	22
23	24	25	26	27	28	29
30	31					

April

SUN	MON	TUE	WED	THU	FRI	SAT
		1	2	3	4	5
6	7	8	9	10	11	12
13	14	15	16	17	18	19
20	21	22	23	24	25	26
27	28	29	30			

May

SUN	MON	TUE	WED	THU	FRI	SAT
				1	2	3
4	5	6	7	8	9	10
11	12	13	14	15	16	17
18	19	20	21	22	23	24
25	26	27	28	29	30	31

June

SUN	MON	TUE	WED	THU	FRI	SAT
1	2	3	4	5	6	7
8	9	10	11	12	13	14
15	16	17	18	19	20	21
22	23	24	25	26	27	28
29	30					

July

SUN	MON	TUE	WED	THU	FRI	SAT
		1	2	3	4	5
6	7	8	9	10	11	12
13	14	15	16	17	18	19
20	21	22	23	24	25	26
27	28	29	30	31		

August

SUN	MON	TUE	WED	THU	FRI	SAT
					1	2
3	4	5	6	7	8	9
10	11	12	13	14	15	16
17	18	19	20	21	22	23
24	25	26	27	28	29	30
31						

September

SUN	MON	TUE	WED	THU	FRI	SAT
	1	2	3	4	5	6
7	8	9	10	11	12	13
14	15	16	17	18	19	20
21	22	23	24	25	26	27
28	29	30				

October

SUN	MON	TUE	WED	THU	FRI	SAT
			1	2	3	4
5	6	7	8	9	10	11
12	13	14	15	16	17	18
19	20	21	22	23	24	25
26	27	28	29	30	31	

November

SUN	MON	TUE	WED	THU	FRI	SAT
						1
2	3	4	5	6	7	8
9	10	11	12	13	14	15
16	17	18	19	20	21	22
23	24	25	26	27	28	29
30						

December

SUN	MON	TUE	WED	THU	FRI	SAT
	1	2	3	4	5	6
7	8	9	10	11	12	13
14	15	16	17	18	19	20
21	22	23	24	25	26	27
28	29	30	31			

2025 *Holidays List*

This planner features US and Canada (CA) legal holidays, important observances of major world religions and some fun days as well. The holidays listed in this planner are accurate to the best of our knowledge and research.

JANUARY
1 New Year's Day
5 National Keto Day
19 National Popcorn Day
20 Martin Luther King Jr. Day
29 Chinese New Year

FEBRUARY
1 Eat Ice Cream for Breakfast Day
2 Groundhog Day, Super Bowl
14 Valentine's Day
15 National Flag of Canada Day
17 Presidents' Day

MARCH
1 First Day of Ramadan
4 Mardi Gras
5 Ash Wednesday, Lent Begins
8 International Women's Day
9 Daylight Saving Time Started
15 Holi
17 St. Patrick's Day
23 Puppy Day
31 Eid al-Fitr

APRIL
1 April Fool's Day
18 Good Friday
19 Passover (first day)
20 Easter Sunday, Look Alike Day
21 Easter Monday(CA)
22 Earth DAY

MAY
1 May Day
5 Cinco de Mayo
11 Mother's Day
17 Armed Forces Day
19 Victoria Day (CA)
20 Be a Millionaire Day
26 Memorial Day

JUNE
2 Shavuot
5 World Environment Day
6 D-Day
7 Eid al-Adha
8 Best Friends Day
14 Flag Day
15 Father's Day
19 Juneteenth
24 Swim a Lap Day
27 Muharram

JULY
1 Canada Day
3 International Plastic Bag Free Day
4 Independence Day
20 Ice Cream Day
27 Parents' Day
30 National Cheesecake Day

AUGUST
3 Sisters' Day
4 Civic Holiday (CA)
7 Purple Heart Day
16 Tell a Joke Day
26 Women's Equality Day

SEPTEMBER
1 Labor Day (USA, CA)
4 The Prophet's Birthday
5 Cheese Pizza Day
7 National Grandparents Day
11 Patriot Day
23 Rosh Hashana
25 Comic Book Day

OCTOBER
2 Yom Kippur
4 Taco Day
7 First Day of Sukkot
13 Columbus Day, Indigenous People's Day, Thanksgiving Day (CA)
16 Boss's Day
18 Chocolate Cupcake Day
21 Diwali
31 Halloween

NOVEMBER
2 Daylight Saving Time Ends
4 Election Day
6 Men Make Dinner Day
11 Veterans Day, Remembrance Day (CA)
20 Universal Children's Day, Use Less Stuff Day
27 Thanksgiving Day
28 Black Friday
30 First Sunday of Advent

DECEMBER
5 Day of the Ninja
7 Pearl Harbor Remembrance Day
12 Gingerbread House Day
15 Chanukah/Hanukkah (first day)
25 Christmas
26 Kwanzaa Begins, Boxing Day (CA, UK)
31 New Year's Eve

01

JANUARY
2025

December

SUN	MON	TUE	WED	THU	FRI	SAT
1	2	3	4	5	6	7
8	9	10	11	12	13	14
15	16	17	18	19	20	21
22	23	24	25	26	27	28
29	30	31				

Major Goals

- [ ] _____
- [ ] _____
- [ ] _____
- [ ] _____
- [ ] _____
- [ ] _____
- [ ] _____
- [ ] _____

Notes

Important Dates

SUNDAY	MONDAY	TUESDAY
05 National Keto Day	06	07
12	13	14
19 National Popcorn Day	20 Martin Luther King Jr. Day	21
26	27	28

February

SUN	MON	TUE	WED	THU	FRI	SAT
						1
2	3	4	5	6	7	8
9	10	11	12	13	14	15
16	17	18	19	20	21	22
23	24	25	26	27	28	

Raise your words, not your voice. It is rain that grows flowers, not thunder.

- Rumi

WEDNESDAY	THURSDAY	FRIDAY	SATURDAY
01 New Year's Day	02	03	04
08	09	10	11
15	16	17	18
22	23	24	25
29 Chinese New Year	30	31	

02

	January					
SUN	MON	TUE	WED	THU	FRI	SAT
			1	2	3	4
5	6	7	8	9	10	11
12	13	14	15	16	17	18
19	20	21	22	23	24	25
26	27	28	29	30	31	

Major Goals

- ☐
- ☐
- ☐
- ☐
- ☐
- ☐
- ☐
- ☐

Notes

Important Dates

SUNDAY	MONDAY	TUESDAY
02 Groundhog Day, Super Bowl	03	04
09	10	11
16	17 Presidents' Day	18
23	24	25

March

SUN	MON	TUE	WED	THU	FRI	SAT
						1
2	3	4	5	6	7	8
9	10	11	12	13	14	15
16	17	18	19	20	21	22
23	24	25	26	27	28	29
30	31					

Don't look for things you aren't ready to find.

\- Unknown

WEDNESDAY	THURSDAY	FRIDAY	SATURDAY
			01 Eat IceCream for Breakfast Day
05	06	07	08
12	13	14 Valentine's Day	15 National Flag of Canada Day
19	20	21	22
26	27	28	

03

MARCH
2025

February

SUN	MON	TUE	WED	THU	FRI	SAT
						1
2	3	4	5	6	7	8
9	10	11	12	13	14	15
16	17	18	19	20	21	22
23	24	25	26	27	28	

Major Goals

- [ ] _____
- [ ] _____
- [ ] _____
- [ ] _____
- [ ] _____
- [ ] _____
- [ ] _____
- [ ] _____

Notes

Important Dates

SUNDAY	MONDAY	TUESDAY
30	31 Eid al Fitr	
02	03	04 Mardi Gras
09 Daylight Saving Time Started	10	11
16	17 St. Patrick's Day	18
23 Puppy Day	24	25

April

SUN	MON	TUE	WED	THU	FRI	SAT
		1	2	3	4	5
6	7	8	9	10	11	12
13	14	15	16	17	18	19
20	21	22	23	24	25	26
27	28	29	30			

Doubt is a killer. You just have to know who you are and what you stand for.

- Jennifer Lopez

WEDNESDAY	THURSDAY	FRIDAY	SATURDAY
			01 First Day of Ramadan
05 Ash Wednesday, Lent Begins	06	07	08 International Women's Day
12	13	14	15 Holi
19	20	21	22
26	27	28	29

04

APRIL
2025

March

SUN	MON	TUE	WED	THU	FRI	SAT
30	31					1
2	3	4	5	6	7	8
9	10	11	12	13	14	15
16	17	18	19	20	21	22
23	24	25	26	27	28	29

Major Goals

- ☐
- ☐
- ☐
- ☐
- ☐
- ☐
- ☐
- ☐

Notes

Important Dates

SUNDAY	MONDAY	TUESDAY
		01 — April Fool's Day
06	07	08
13	14	15
20 — Easter Sunday, Look Alike Day	21 — Easter Monday (CA)	22 — Earth DAY
27	28	29

May

SUN	MON	TUE	WED	THU	FRI	SAT
				1	2	3
4	5	6	7	8	9	10
11	12	13	14	15	16	17
18	19	20	21	22	23	24
25	26	27	28	29	30	31

If you don't like being a doormat then get off the floor.

- Al Anon

WEDNESDAY	THURSDAY	FRIDAY	SATURDAY
02	03	04	05
09	10	11	12
16	17	18 Good Friday	19 Passover (first day)
23	24	25	26
30			

05

MAY
2025

April

SUN	MON	TUE	WED	THU	FRI	SAT
		1	2	3	4	5
6	7	8	9	10	11	12
13	14	15	16	17	18	19
20	21	22	23	24	25	26
27	28	29	30			

Major Goals

- ☐ _____
- ☐ _____
- ☐ _____
- ☐ _____
- ☐ _____
- ☐ _____
- ☐ _____
- ☐ _____

Notes

Important Dates

SUNDAY	MONDAY	TUESDAY
04	05 Cinco de Mayo	06
11 Mother's Day	12	13
18	19 Victoria Day (CA)	20 Be a Millionaire Day
25	26 Memorial Day	27

Jun

SUN	MON	TUE	WED	THU	FRI	SAT
1	2	3	4	5	6	7
8	9	10	11	12	13	14
15	16	17	18	19	20	21
22	23	24	25	26	27	28
29	30					

I know God will not give me anything I can't handle.
I just wish that He didn't trust me so much.

\- Mother Teresa

WEDNESDAY	THURSDAY	FRIDAY	SATURDAY
	01 May Day	02	03
07	08	09	10
14	15	16	17 Armed Forces Day
21	22	23	24
28	29	30	31

06

JUNE
2025

May

SUN	MON	TUE	WED	THU	FRI	SAT
				1	2	3
4	5	6	7	8	9	10
11	12	13	14	15	16	17
18	19	20	21	22	23	24
25	26	27	28	29	30	31

Major Goals

- ☐ _____
- ☐ _____
- ☐ _____
- ☐ _____
- ☐ _____
- ☐ _____
- ☐ _____
- ☐ _____

Notes

Important Dates

SUNDAY	MONDAY	TUESDAY
01	02 Shavuot	03
08 Best Friends Day	09	10
15 Father's Day	16	17
22	23	24 Swim a Lap Day
29	30	

July

SUN	MON	TUE	WED	THU	FRI	SAT
		1	2	3	4	5
6	7	8	9	10	11	12
13	14	15	16	17	18	19
20	21	22	23	24	25	26
27	28	29	30	31		

You will succeed, just keep going.

- Unknown

WEDNESDAY	THURSDAY	FRIDAY	SATURDAY
04	05 World Environment Day	06 D-Day	07 Eid al-Adha
11	12	13	14 Flag Day
18	19 Juneteenth	20	21
25	26	27 Muharram	28

07

JULY
2025

June

SUN	MON	TUE	WED	THU	FRI	SAT
1	2	3	4	5	6	7
8	9	10	11	12	13	14
15	16	17	18	19	20	21
22	23	24	25	26	27	28
29	30					

Major Goals

- ☐ _____
- ☐ _____
- ☐ _____
- ☐ _____
- ☐ _____
- ☐ _____
- ☐ _____
- ☐ _____

Notes

Important Dates

SUNDAY	MONDAY	TUESDAY
		01 Canada Day
06	07	08
13	14	15
20 Ice Cream Day	21	22
27 Parents' Day	28	29

August

SUN	MON	TUE	WED	THU	FRI	SAT
					1	2
3	4	5	6	7	8	9
10	11	12	13	14	15	16
17	18	19	20	21	22	23
24	25	26	27	28	29	30
31						

Stop wearing your wishbone where your backbone ought to be.

\- Elizabeth Gilbert

WEDNESDAY	THURSDAY	FRIDAY	SATURDAY
02	03 International Plastic Bag Free Day	04 Independence Day	05
09	10	11	12
16	17	18	19
23	24	25	26
30 National Cheesecake Day	31		

08

AUGUST
2025

July

SUN	MON	TUE	WED	THU	FRI	SAT
		1	2	3	4	5
6	7	8	9	10	11	12
13	14	15	16	17	18	19
20	21	22	23	24	25	26
27	28	29	30	31		

Major Goals

- ☐ _____
- ☐ _____
- ☐ _____
- ☐ _____
- ☐ _____
- ☐ _____
- ☐ _____
- ☐ _____

Notes

Important Dates

SUNDAY	MONDAY	TUESDAY
31		
03 — Sisters' Day	04 — Civic Holiday (CA)	05
10	11	12
17	18	19
24	25	26 — Women's Equality Day

September

SUN	MON	TUE	WED	THU	FRI	SAT
		1	2	3	4	5	6
7	8	9	10	11	12	13
14	15	16	17	18	19	20
21	22	23	24	25	26	27
28	29	30				

A man's got to do what a man's got to do.
A woman must do what he can't.

- Rhonda Hansome

WEDNESDAY	THURSDAY	FRIDAY	SATURDAY
		01	02
06	07 Purple Heart Day	08	09
13	14	15	16 Tell a Joke Day
20	21	22	23
27	28	29	30

09

SEPTEMBER
2025

August

SUN	MON	TUE	WED	THU	FRI	SAT
					1	2
3	4	5	6	7	8	9
10	11	12	13	14	15	16
17	18	19	20	21	22	23
24	25	26	27	28	29	30
31						

Major Goals

- ☐
- ☐
- ☐
- ☐
- ☐
- ☐
- ☐
- ☐

Notes

Important Dates

SUNDAY	MONDAY	TUESDAY
	01 Labor Day (USA, CA)	02
07 National Grandparents Day	08	09
14	15	16
21	22	23 Rosh Hashana
28	29	30

October

SUN	MON	TUE	WED	THU	FRI	SAT
			1	2	3	4
5	6	7	8	9	10	11
12	13	14	15	16	17	18
19	20	21	22	23	24	25
26	27	28	29	30	31	

You Only Live Once. You Might As Well As A Badass!

– Anon

WEDNESDAY	THURSDAY	FRIDAY	SATURDAY
03	04 The Prophet's Birthday	05 Cheese Pizza Day	06
10	11 Patriot Day	12	13
17	18	19	20
24	25 Comic Book Day	26	27

10

OCTOBER
2025

September

SUN	MON	TUE	WED	THU	FRI	SAT
	1	2	3	4	5	6
7	8	9	10	11	12	13
14	15	16	17	18	19	20
21	22	23	24	25	26	27
28	29	30				

Major Goals

- ☐ _____
- ☐ _____
- ☐ _____
- ☐ _____
- ☐ _____
- ☐ _____
- ☐ _____
- ☐ _____

Notes

Important Dates

SUNDAY	MONDAY	TUESDAY
05	06	07 — First Day of Sukkot
12	13 — Columbus Day, Indigenous People's Day, Thanksgiving Day (CA)	14
19	20	21 — Diwali
26	27	28

November

SUN	MON	TUE	WED	THU	FRI	SAT
						1
2	3	4	5	6	7	8
9	10	11	12	13	14	15
16	17	18	19	20	21	22
23	24	25	26	27	28	29
30						

Failure Is The Opportunity To Being Again More Intelligently.

- Henry Ford

WEDNESDAY	THURSDAY	FRIDAY	SATURDAY
01	02 Yom Kippur	03	04 Taco Day
08	09	10	11
15	16 Boss's Day	17	18 Chocolate Cupcake Day
22	23	24	25
29	30	31 Halloween	

11

NOVEMBER
2025

October
SUN	MON	TUE	WED	THU	FRI	SAT
			1	2	3	4
5	6	7	8	9	10	11
12	13	14	15	16	17	18
19	20	21	22	23	24	25
26	27	28	29	30	31	

Major Goals

- ☐ _____
- ☐ _____
- ☐ _____
- ☐ _____
- ☐ _____
- ☐ _____
- ☐ _____
- ☐ _____

Notes

Important Dates

SUNDAY	MONDAY	TUESDAY
30 First Sunday of Advent		
02 Daylight Saving Time Ends	**03**	**04** Election Day
09	**10**	**11** Veterans Day, Remembrance Day (CA)
16	**17**	**18**
23	**24**	**25**

December

SUN	MON	TUE	WED	THU	FRI	SAT
		1	2	3	4	5	6
7	8	9	10	11	12	13
14	15	16	17	18	19	20
21	22	23	24	25	26	27
28	29	30	31			

You're Allowed To Scream. You're Allowed To Cry. But Do Not Give Up.

- Unknown

WEDNESDAY	THURSDAY	FRIDAY	SATURDAY
			01
05	06 Men Make Dinner Day	07	08
12	13	14	15
19	20 Universal Children's Day, Use Less Stuff Day	21	22
26	27 Thanksgiving Day	28 Black Friday	29

12

DECEMBER
2025

November

SUN	MON	TUE	WED	THU	FRI	SAT
						1
2	3	4	5	6	7	8
9	10	11	12	13	14	15
16	17	18	19	20	21	22
23	24	25	26	27	28	29
30						

Major Goals

- ☐ _____
- ☐ _____
- ☐ _____
- ☐ _____
- ☐ _____
- ☐ _____
- ☐ _____
- ☐ _____

Notes

Important Dates

SUNDAY	MONDAY	TUESDAY
	01	02
07 Pearl Harbor Remembrance Day	08	09
14	15 Chanukah/Hanukkah (first day)	16
21	22	23
28	29	30

January

SUN	MON	TUE	WED	THU	FRI	SAT
				1	2	3
4	5	6	7	8	9	10
11	12	13	14	15	16	17
18	19	20	21	22	23	24
25	26	27	28	29	30	31

The Woman Who Does Not Required Validation From Anyone Is The Most Feared Individual On The Planet.

- Mohadesa Najumi

WEDNESDAY	THURSDAY	FRIDAY	SATURDAY
03	04	05 Day of the Ninja	06
10	11	12 Gingerbread House Day	13
17	18	19	20
24	25 Christmas	26 Kwanzaa Begins, Boxing Day (CA, UK)	27
31 New Year's Eve			

Notes

Notes

Notes

Made in the USA
Coppell, TX
10 September 2020